For Georgia Rose

First edition 2009

Library of Congress Cataloging-in-Publication Data is available.

Library of Congress Catalog Card Number 2008939935

ISBN 978-0-7636-3597-8

2 4 6 8 10 9 7 5 3 1

Printed in China

This book was typeset in Alghera.
The illustrations were done in watercolor and ink.

Candlewick Press
99 Dover Street
Somerville, Massachusetts 02144

visit us at www.candlewick.com

Miss Mingo
and the Fire Drill

Jamie Harper

Candlewick Press

"It's fire safety week!" Miss Mingo announced to her class one Monday morning in early October. "We'll be learning what to do in case there's a fire."

"My grammy had a fire!" Alligator said. "It was in her frying pan. The smoke detector went off, and it was *really* scary, and my French toast got burned, but I ate it anyway."

Everyone agreed it sounded very scary.

Panda started barking.

Elephant trumpeted.

Bird growled.

Animals use a number of defense mechanisms to protect themselves from danger. Many of them make loud, harsh sounds to scare off predators.

And Monkey honked. "I'm afraid of *smoke detectors*," he admitted.

"What's wrong with your nose?" asked Bird.

When danger threatens, the proboscis monkey honks loudly, and its large, fleshy nose swells and turns red.

But before Monkey could answer, the room started to shake.

Elephant was stomping his feet and flapping his ears.
"I'm afraid of fire trucks!" he cried.

Frightened elephants stomp their feet, flap their ears, and trumpet. Younger elephants may push their ears way out to the side to appear more threatening.

"Now, now, let's simmer down," said Miss Mingo. "I know fire can be scary. Just thinking about it makes me want to hide behind my friends. But I know I have to follow the rules when there's danger. So today we have a visitor coming who will teach us how to be safe and well prepared."

Flamingos move in large, tightly packed flocks, making it easier for them to spot lone predators.

At that moment,
a very big bear
entered the room.

"Good morning!" he roared.

Snake hissed loudly and puffed up his body as much as he could.

When threatened, the hognose snake inflates its body to resemble a cobra. It also flattens its head and hisses.

Pig darted away from the bear and
dove under Miss Mingo's desk.
"No need to be afraid," Miss Mingo reassured them.
"It's just Chief Grizzly under all that gear."

A startled pig will run away
and then quickly turn around to face
whatever frightened it. If necessary, it will charge
its enemy and use its tusks to attack.

Miss Mingo

The chief removed his mask. "Firefighters need
to wear all of this to be well protected," he said.

"It's called turnout gear,"
Frog said proudly.
"It can weigh up
to seventy pounds."

It didn't take long for the class to warm up to Chief Grizzly.

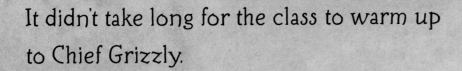

"What do you do when the smoke detector sounds?"
he asked the class.

"Get out and stay out!" yelled Frog.

"Right again," said the chief.
"Does anyone know what to do
if your clothes catch on fire?"
Everyone knew
the answer.

STOP!

DROP!

ROLL!

Miss Mingo promised Chief Grizzly that
they would work on their technique.

On Tuesday morning, Miss Mingo explained
that sometime soon there would be a fire drill.

"When?" asked Narwhal.

"I don't know," answered Miss Mingo.
"But don't worry. We will practice,
and we will be ready."
She listed the steps that they would
need to follow.

Stop everything.

Get in line with
a buddy.

No talking!

Follow the primary
route out of the
building.

Go to a designated
spot outside and
line up.

First they practiced lining up.
Alligator insisted on being the leader.
Koala brought along a snack.
And everyone was talking.

"Remember," said Miss Mingo, "everything stays here in the room."

"Even my eucalyptus?" asked Koala. "I can't leave it behind!"

Koala was so upset that he started rubbing his chest and growling.

"Peeeeeeeeeu!" exclaimed Alligator. "What's that smell?" She dropped Koala's hand and ran to the end of the line.

Koalas howl and wail when they are upset. In some aggressive encounters, the male koala rubs his chest. The glands there release a strong, musty odor.

"Oh, my," said Miss Mingo, opening up a window.
"Why don't we practice some more—outside?"

"Today we will take the *primary route* to get outside," Miss Mingo said as they left the room. "That's the most direct way out and the closest to a building's exit."

"The *secondary route*," announced Frog, "is just another way we can go in case we can't use the first one."

Miss Mingo gave him a nod. There was lots of noise as the class made its way through the halls.

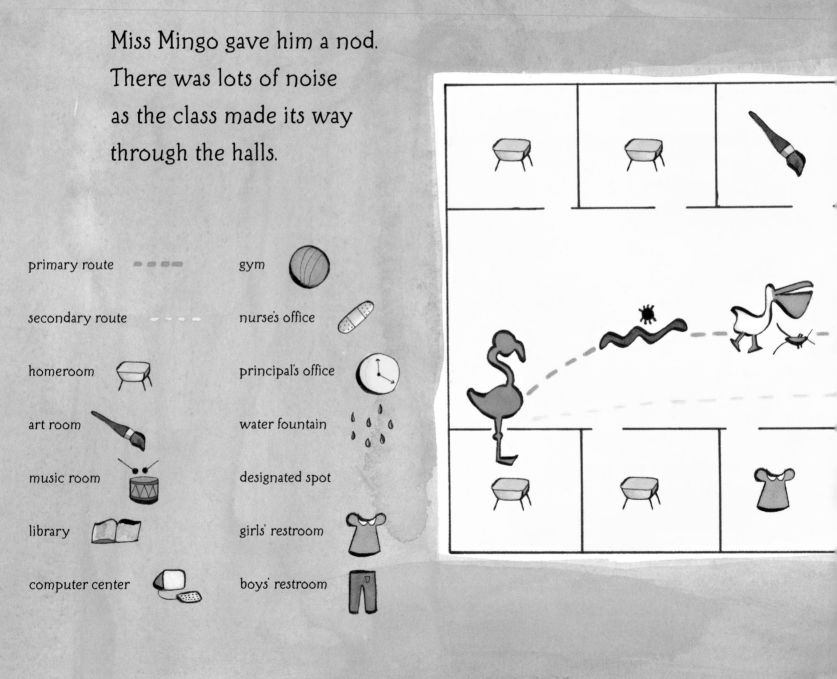

primary route	– – – –	gym	
secondary route	- - - -	nurse's office	
homeroom		principal's office	
art room		water fountain	
music room		designated spot	
library		girls' restroom	
computer center		boys' restroom	

EXIT

EXIT

Finally, Miss Mingo's class made it
to the meeting spot outside.

Miss Mingo called each student by name.
When Panda didn't answer, she scanned the school yard.
It didn't take Miss Mingo long to spot her wedged
in a tree, all curled up.

"Panda, why aren't you in line?"

"I'm scared," Panda said. "What if I'm all alone in the bathroom when the alarm goes off?"

"No one will be left behind," said Miss Mingo. "The teachers and firefighters will check the whole school. They'll tell us when it's safe to go back inside."

A panda escapes danger by running away or climbing a tree. If trapped, it growls and swipes with its paws— or simply covers its face and and curls up into a ball.

On Wednesday, Miss Dillo, the lunch monitor, came to eat with the class while Miss Mingo ate in the teachers' lounge.

Suddenly a loud sound ripped through the classroom.
"Excuse me," said Hippo, wiping his nose.

"It's the fire drill!" yelled Cockroach.

"No, no, it was just a sneeze!" cried Hippo.
But no one heard him.

Giraffe was so frightened that he tipped over his chair.
"Stop everything . . . please," Miss Dillo said.
Cockroach was hissing loudly, which
made Centipede mad.

If faced with danger, giraffes can deliver a deadly kick
with their front legs—powerful enough to kill a lion.
Their speed also helps them to escape.

Cockroaches attack other insects by
kicking with their legs, which are
covered with sharp bristles.

Centipedes defend themselves by pinching with their
back legs or biting with their front fangs. They can
escape a predator by simply shedding the legs that
are being held captive. New ones will grow in soon.

"Stop!" Hippo yelled. "It isn't the fire drill!"

"It's a real fire?" Alligator screamed.

Miss Dillo rolled herself into a ball.

Alligator thrashed her tail wildly.

THWACK!

A mother alligator defends her hatchlings against predators by hissing, chomping her jaws, and using her most powerful weapon, a thrashing tail.

To stay safe, the three-banded armadillo rolls up into a grapefruit-size ball, completely enclosing its body within its leathery plates or "armor."

Everyone stopped to watch
Miss Dillo fly across the room —
right into Hippo's mouth!

Pelican smacked
him on the back,
and out popped
Miss Dillo.

She rolled out of the classroom just
as Miss Mingo returned from lunch.
"Mercy me!" Miss Mingo cried.

Friday morning, students trickled into the classroom.
Miss Mingo reviewed all they had learned about fire
safety one more time. During the morning meeting,
a siren blasted and bright red lights flashed.
"It's here!" hollered Pig.

"It's the fire drill!"
Octopus cried.
He squirted a
cloud of ink
into the room.

An octopus squirts a cloud
of ink to confuse its enemies
and then dashes away under
cover of the smoky screen.

But the class stayed calm. Narwhal helped
some of his classmates to the doorway, where
students began to line up with their buddies.

Miss Mingo led her class out of the room and down the hallway. Everyone protected their ears from the loud sound. There was no talking. There was no running. And no one stopped at the cubbies (although Alligator tried).

The students were just about to exit the building when they found Chief Grizzly blocking the entrance with a sign that read FIRE! He smiled and then winked, and they knew that this was a special test.

EXIT

FiRe!

Frog nodded, and the class filed out using the secondary route.